W9-BZW-609

Visiting the Elderly

AN ESSENTIAL PARISH MINISTRY

✍ DEDICATION ℘

This book is dedicated to my parents, Anesa and Kalil Jabour, now deceased, who taught me at an early age to respect persons of all ages. They inspired me to remember our family history and ancestry and to make a valued connection with our past as it touches the present and propels us into the future. I learned early in life to listen, to value continuity of life, and to respect our elders. Ma and Pa lived a life of faith in God and passed the gift on to me. I am forever grateful.

Twenty-Third Publications
A Division of Bayard
One Montauk Avenue, Suite 200
New London, CT 06320
(860) 437-3012 or (800) 321-0411
www.23rdpublications.com

ISBN 978-1-58595-631-9
Library of Congress Catalog Card Number: 2007930687
Printed in the U.S.A.

❧ Contents ❧

ACKNOWLEDGMENTS   IV

FOREWORD   VI

INTRODUCTION   1

CHAPTER ONE
   The Aging Person: A Gift from God   8

CHAPTER TWO
   The Ministry of Visiting Elders   19

CHAPTER THREE
   The Visiting Experience   36

CHAPTER FOUR
   Response to Spiritual Needs   54

CHAPTER FIVE
   Suffering and Dying with Jesus   65

CONCLUSION   78

✥ ACKNOWLEDGMENTS ❧

Many people have encouraged me through the years. Their support and affirmation make this book possible. In particular I mention:

» My brothers and sisters. As the youngest of seven children, I received much encouragement from them to do my best and reach for the stars.

» My Adrian Dominican Congregation, especially the many older sisters with whom I shared community. They were outstanding examples of how to age gracefully.

» My coworkers, especially at St. Theresa Home, Catholic Social Service of Southwest Ohio, and Bayley Place, who epitomized mutual love and care for those we served.

» Members of the LifeLearn Program who patiently listened to my stories and encouraged me to put them in writing so others could appreciate and value the gifts and grace of aging.

» Father Bob Hater who encouraged me to write my life-giving experiences with older adults, who never gave up on me, and who showed me how to express my experiences more clearly.

» Adrienne Walsh who encouraged me to share my stories and expertise in helping others understand and appreciate our aging members better.

» Denise Donnelly and Lisa Caminiti for their expert advice in the area of technology and their patience with my "computer" questions. They read the questions on my face before I could articulate them.

◄§ FOREWORD §►

In Genesis, Yahweh took dust from the earth and created us in God's image (Gen 1:26). Our story testifies to the living image of the creator. As such, our story becomes a holy of holies, containing traces of the divine image, analogous to the Holy of Holies in the Hebrew Scriptures and the Eucharist in Christianity.

When I read Sr. Jeanette Jabour's book I entered the sacred space of her life, that of her family, and the thousands of seniors that she has blessed through her ministry. The book is the fruit of over forty years of caring for the elderly and dying, as a friend, counselor, and pastoral minister with families, social agencies, and retirement homes. As such, it teems with academic knowledge, pastoral skills, and years of experience. Many books speak of the elderly, but rarely do we find one of such depth.

There is more to the book than knowledge, skills, and experience. It is a wisdom book, rooted in a profound regard for the sanctity of elder persons, seen as gifts from God. Words about the elderly are wonderful, but experience with them is even more profound. I experienced Sr. Jeanette's love of the elderly in her relationship with my mother. For years before Mom died at ninety-one, she and Jeanette were friends. I witnessed their interaction many times and the respect they had for each other. When Mom became seriously ill, Jeanette was beside her at home, in the retirement facility, and at the hospital. As her last hours approached, Jeanette stayed with Mom and the family until we left the hospital room for a few moments to get something to eat. When we returned, Mom had died.

Over many years, Sr. Jeanette learned fruitful lessons about ministering with the sick and dying, most important of which is the need to be present to dying persons and their families. She was there for Mom, our family, and me. For her love and concern, I am eternally grateful.

I was blessed when I read her book. She begins with reflections on the need to appreciate older adults as gifts from God. She indicates that when we are with them, they often give us more than we give them. This is an important lesson in our hectic world, where we easily miss important life moments in our desire to do it all.

Grounding her remarks in the sacredness of the elderly person, Sr. Jeanette gives us excellent advice on visiting and ministering to the elderly. Here, her experience manifests itself as she reflects on the value of a parish minister's response to the elderly person's past contributions. She stresses listening skills, as she develops her remarks on visiting the elderly in their homes, care facilities, and hospitals. She offers specific ideas on how to set up a parish care program. Her comments provide invaluable help for parish ministers.

The significance of praying with elders and attending to their spiritual needs is in the forefront of what she writes. In this regard, she stresses memories as a fruitful place to begin when dealing with older adults. Toward the end of her book, Sr. Jeanette connects her previous remarks with Jesus' life and teaching, especially his suffering and death. Relying on her deep Christian faith and extensive experience, she knows how to link human suffering to the suffering of Jesus. In so doing, Sr. Jeanette underlines the significance of faith in the face of sickness and death. She also discusses the sacrament of anointing as a means for preparing an elderly person for eternal life.

I felt honored when Sr. Jeanette asked me to write this Foreword. In her wonderful book, she takes readers on a journey through the stories of holy people who have lived, celebrated, and suffered in this world, and who are now with God for all eternity. This book is a sacred journey filled with wisdom, practical skills, knowledge, and the basics necessary for fruitful ministry with elders.

Rev. Robert J. Hater, Ph.D.
Professor Emeritus, University of Dayton
Professor of Pastoral and Systematic Theology,
Athenaeum of Ohio

∽§ INTRODUCTION §∾

My parents were raised in the Middle East when Lebanon was a Christian country. As a child, I heard more scripture-based stories than nursery rhymes. And so, relating the events of life to spiritual stories comes naturally to me. Because of my earlier experiences, it is easy for me to incorporate a spiritual element into ordinary events. Stories of the lives of most people are ordinary events. These stories must be told to assure continuity of life and history.

Sharing one's personal story has a healing effect on both the storyteller and the listener. The event marks a sacred moment in time. Telling a story provides elders with a vehicle for leaving behind a legacy as they move forward in life, a legacy that benefits both the elder speaker and the listener. It helps the elder realize her or his life was not lived in vain. Relating the story in the context of prayer brings an accompanying blessing with it.

In Luke 10:27–37, a scholar of the law asks Jesus "What must I do to inherit eternal life?" And Jesus asked him "What is written in the law?" The scholar replied "You shall love the Lord, your God, with all your heart, all your being, all your strength, and all your mind, and your neighbor as yourself." Jesus replied "You have answered correctly; do this and you shall live." And the scholar said "And who is my neighbor?" And Jesus replied with a story, the familiar parable of the Good Samaritan. Jesus placed value on storytelling by using a simple story to explain a profound truth.

Everyone has a story to tell, but not everyone has an opportunity to tell it. Nor does everyone have the availability of a willing and interested listener. Most parishes do provide the service of eucharistic ministry to the sick and homebound, and this offers the opportunity for storytelling and listening as well. Engaging in conversation following a period of quiet reflection is a good time to elicit a story. This does prolong the time spent with the person, but it is a worthwhile activity. It satisfies the need for some elderly parishioners to share their stories and to feel connected to the parish community.

In "Blessings of Age: A Pastoral Message on Growing Older within the Faith Community," a statement of the U.S. bishops written in 1999, the bishops offer a message about the importance of ministering to elders. They remind us that the spiritual growth of the aging person is affected by the community and also affects the community. It says that "aging demands the attention of the entire Church." It further states that "how the faith community relates to its older members...is a sign of the community's spiritual health and maturity."

Spiritual health and maturity involve the way in which individuals live their lives, grow in their relationship with others, and move toward a greater understanding and appreciation of God. Each person is involved in a spiritual growth process. As members of the Church, we walk through the process together. Encouragement to grow spiritually is given to us along the way. No one should travel the road alone.

Through one's early and middle years, finding someone with whom to walk the spiritual path comes easily for most people. But as a person ages, the number of persons involved in one's personal life often diminishes, especially when it comes to spiritual growth. Many are left to find their own resources. A visiting ministry in a parish helps to satisfy this need.

The challenge in many parishes is to reach out to those elders within parish boundaries who are not on any sick lists or on lists of hospital discharges, yet are no longer able to attend parish services and activities. They are often forgotten. But they too have a story to tell. They too need a contact from the parish community, someone who will listen, someone who can bring a touch of sacredness to a life situation.

Over the past thirty years, hundreds of older adults have shared stories from their lives with me. Each person's story is unique, yet common threads run through them. Many of the threads center on love, forgiveness, personal presence, and faith. Each story carries a message for all who are willing to listen. The ministry of visiting elders, through a parish or through any other vehicle, provides the milieu for older adults to share their stories, to pray with others, and to remain a vital part of the parish community.

Each story reflects a real-life situation. Each story occurred regardless of or in spite of the challenges of life. Physical challenges often accompany chronological aging.

However, with growth in years, spirituality and wisdom deepen and become more prominent. The spiritual aspects of aging continue to grow even as other aspects of life decline. The spiritual aspects of life are chief contributors to many decisions and choices made in later life, which are valued by those who make them and influential for those who listen to them. Through years of spiritual growth, elders are more apt to find God and anchor themselves in God in small unspectacular ways and events. A long life allows persons to put their experiences into some perspective. They learn that it is easy to find God in the spectacular, but it takes great faith and years of wisdom to discover God in the ordinary, daily events of life.

The information offered in this handbook serves as a guide to those who minister to and with elders. The topics explored offer support in understanding aging persons. The information provided can assist ministers in making a pastoral visit meaningful, both for the visitor and the person visited. The handbook contains five chapters, and illustrative stories support each topic. Each chapter ends with appropriate points for reflection and action.

Chapter One, "The Aging Person: A Gift from God," offers many reasons to appreciate older adults. Honoring a lifetime of experience and remembering life stories are gestures of affirmation for those who previously attained noteworthy goals, either through a paid position or by maintaining a well-run household and family. This chapter emphasizes that a quality life is desirable for all persons of all ages. A quality life is the privilege of each person created by God. The section on recognizing changes in later years reminds us that although changes occur all through life, they are generally more noticeable in the later years. These changes can be overpowering and bring stress. But change can also bring growth. Moving to a different living situation, for example, is a major change for many older adults. Though the move can be stressful it may also offer the opportunity to meet new friends, participate in life-giving activities, and enjoy three good meals a day. Consequently, in spite of experiencing change and stress, the person grows in better health and happiness. And finally, through a respect for and appreciation of mutual ministry, as visitor and person visited enter into a relationship, the one ministered to also becomes a minister. This happens through the sharing of life values and faith experiences.

Chapter Two concentrates on the ministry of visiting elders. Some reasons for visiting are to bring hope and comfort to the lonely and to offer gratitude for years of participation in the parish. A visitor brings hope and comfort to the lonely through active listening and by affirming the elder as a person, showing that the elder is worthy of time and capable of building relationships. A visitor offers comfort by walking with the elder on her or his journey with God. Many older adults have spent years participating in the life of the parish. Through a pastoral visit, a visitor expresses gratitude for the elder's membership and participation. This confirms that the older adult is still connected to the parish. Chapter Two also offers listening skills and communication tips, which facilitate the visitor's conversations with elders.

Chapter Three explores the visiting experience in more detail. Part One provides guidelines for visiting elders. General guidelines are given along with specific guidelines to be followed when visiting elders living at home, persons living in care facilities, or during hospital visitations. The guidelines are extensive and can apply to visiting elders in any of the above settings. Following the guidelines are communication tips, both verbal and nonverbal. Part Two, setting up a parish visiting program, discusses the responsibilities of a coordinator and of parish visitors. It also describes various aspects of the organization of a visiting program.

Chapter Four, "Response to Spiritual Needs," is divided into four parts. Part One, praying with elders, discusses the ministry of prayer. Through prayer, God is brought into the conversation. Prayer invites a reflective presence and a quiet mutual respect. Part Two, refocusing energy, is helpful for allowing an elder to express feelings of pain and to recognize accompanying losses. Lingering issues in Part Three can be a deterrent to spiritual growth and raise questions about the elder's relationship with God. Questions arise as to whether God understands and loves them enough to forgive. Such issues include experiencing suffering and growth, sharing memories, a need for reconciliation, and welcoming God's graces into one's life.

Chapter Five offers reflections on suffering and dying with Jesus. They recall Jesus as the model of suffering and discuss the power to choose in the midst of suffering. They also help the person face the reality of death. The final section offers vital information for the Christian on the sacrament of anointing.

Having a knowledge and understanding of some of the experiences of the aging process and of the changes that accompany the aging process make the visit more productive for both prayer and conversation. Understanding the aging process helps create an atmosphere of mutual respect and allows the experience to be meaningful to both the elder visited and the person visiting. Allowing our good and gracious God into the process creates an atmosphere for growth to occur in all who share life through these ministries.

May God's blessing be with all who participate in these vital ministries.

The Aging Person: A Gift from God

Charlie lives in an assisted living facility. He is ninety-two years old and has limited vision. He also has Parkinson's disease. Charlie has no living immediate family, but a niece assumes some responsibility for his care. During his working years Charlie was a bartender, and in his words "the best bartender in town." He was friendly and kind to all his customers. He listened to their stories and tried to respond in a caring way. During the later years of his life, Charlie's niece collected his social security check monthly and sent a check to the facility for his rent. He really did not know exactly how much money he had. He never inquired about finances, because he did not want to lose the only family contact he had.

One day his niece suffered a debilitating heart attack. In the midst of suffering the loss of his only relative, Charlie wondered about his own security. Would he be able to remain at the facility?

The social worker at the facility eventually introduced Charlie to a lawyer who straightened out Charlie's financial affairs and kept him informed about his finances. Charlie learned he had enough money to buy some much-needed clothing. Much of the shaking that accompanies Parkinson's eased. Eventually Charlie resumed an aspect of his previous role as bartender, not by tending bar, but by visiting and listening to the stories of other residents, and by offering words of encouragement and affirmation to as many as possible. Charlie truly understood and appreciated all the people that came into his life, and reciprocated care and friendship to them.

Appreciating Older Adults

Charlie appreciated other persons for who they were, and his sense of appreciation facilitated all the relationships he formed throughout his life. In this section, general information on aging will assist in understanding older adults better. A greater understanding of elders will assist those who visit and pray with them. Some pastoral visitors visit elders regularly and are comfortable in doing so. Some visit elders on a regular basis, but are uncomfortable about carrying on a con-

versation. Some would like to visit elders in a parish, but
don't do so because of their level of discomfort. Reasons for
discomfort can be age differences, or impatience with the
memory- or hearing-impaired, or from not knowing where to
begin a conversation with someone who is not an acquaintance. Not knowing what a person's interests are can also be a
deterrent to carrying on a conversation.

Elders that spend much time alone welcome a listening
ear and an interested, friendly person. Some older adults
have been parishioners in the same parish for many years.
Others may have moved from time to time and are aging in
a new parish with new parishioners. However, all have had
many experiences and deserve to be recognized.

A Gesture of Affirmation

Honoring a lifetime of experience is a gesture of affirmation,
one that contributes to the well-being of an individual at any
age. An acknowledgment of life experiences is especially
affirming for those who previously attained noteworthy
goals and are no longer in the active world. Affirmation is a
way of recognizing a person's God-given gifts, which, con-
trary to popular belief, do not diminish or disappear as a person ages. Personal gifts develop as they are used. Many elders
continue to recognize and use their gifts. Some use them
best when called forth by other persons and groups in their
lives. Persons who used well-developed personal skills in
their earlier years often redirect these skills to new situations.
They are simply used in new ways.

Henrietta spent many years working as a secretary, filing and keeping order for others in an office. In her later years, she experienced some memory impairment. This necessitated a move to a nursing facility. A visitor from her parish knew Henrietta's background and shared it with the Activities Director, who later found activities that involved sorting and putting items in order. These activities came naturally to Henrietta and she once again felt she was serving others.

The transfer of gifts can also occur in activities of faith. Adults find meaning in life activities and in faith when there is an opportunity to express it to others. They welcome opportunities to use what they know and what they do to express their faith. Parishes that encourage adults to experience new opportunities to express their faith provide a service for growth in faith. This often occurs while honoring a lifetime of experience in older adults and affirming their years of lived wisdom. Regardless of the person's current condition or situation, acquired wisdom exists. While conversing with a person at length, such wisdom becomes obvious and is easily observed. However, when the ability to converse is limited, due to memory loss or other impairments, the ability for a listener to recognize acquired wisdom may be limited. Yet, the elder has still lived a full life and has many wisdom stories hidden within. With a little patience and some skill in listening and conversing, bits of wisdom will emerge. Just because a person's memory has failed, doesn't mean that

that person's life experience has disappeared. What disappears is the memory of parts of the former life. This brings up another vital part of honoring a lifetime of experience, and that is the experience of remembering life stories.

Remembering Life Stories

During his early years, Jim enjoyed carving wood objects as a hobby. In later years, when illness prevented him from remaining independent, he moved into a long-term care facility. Because of his physical immobility, many assumed he was incapable of participating in activities. However, a visitor from his former parish remembered his talent of carving and encouraged him to resume the art. Jim resumed his carving activity by carving beautiful canes out of fallen tree branches and sharing these with other residents in the facility. He was so happy with his activity that he actually gained back some of his physical strength. Meanwhile, he made numerous new friends by sharing his classy canes with them.

All that happened in a person's life remains part of them forever. Remembering their life stories and allowing elders to recall their stories is another way of honoring their life experience. The stories of persons who have been active leaders in the parish and community are often known and recognized. As they grow older, it is reaffirming to them to recall their stories. It is also reaffirming when the listener reflects and remembers portions of the elder's story. However, many older adults were not necessarily active leaders outside their immediate family. These persons also have a lifetime story to tell. They also lived full lives of service in some way, either to family or to the parish or community. Many long to have their story heard but are not sure who will provide the listening ear or the caring heart. Making the connection for meaningful storytelling is a gift that interested persons can give to elders in their parish. Honoring another's experience, affirming their years of wisdom, and remembering their stories contribute to promoting quality life for them in their later years.

Promoting a Quality Life

A quality life is the privilege of each person created by God. One definition of a quality life is that the situation has a degree of excellence, the best it can be for a particular situation. Some persons, due to age-related situations and conditions, are unable to maintain a quality life for themselves. They depend on others to provide it for them. Participating in the ministries of visiting and praying with elders is one way of promoting quality of life for them. Other ways of honoring a person's lifetime of experience include being a good listener and being comfortable in the presence of another, regardless of the situation or condition. These actions assure the person that they are still important to the parish and community, that their prayers, presence, and suffering is recognized and appreciated, and that they are a vital part of the entire Church of God.

The visitor can assure the elder that if they need something to improve their current quality of life, he or she will assist in satisfying insofar as possible. Of course, not every need can be satisfied, and this need not detract from the quality of a person's life. A quality life is the best it can be for each particular situation. It helps to be able to recognize that many situations and conditions are created because of the changes that occur in a person's life, particularly in the later years.

Recognizing Change

Changes occur all through life at every age, but they are generally more noticeable in the later years when major changes occur more often. Major changes can produce stress but can also bring growth, depending on one's response to them. All of life centers around change. For example, elders spend years building up relationships with people in their neighborhoods and are comfortable with them. A change in their condition may necessitate a move to another neighborhood or city. This is a major change that may necessitate building new relationships with doctors, dentists, and other professionals; a different hairdresser or barber; a new grocery store; a different mailperson. The neighbors and entire neighborhood may be unfamiliar, as well as the local shopping area. These and many other changes challenge any trust level the elders may have built up from their former neighborhoods. They sense a loss of control over their own decision-making powers. Moving to another neighborhood is a major change, but other changes also, especially in the life of elders, need to be recognized.

> Betty lived in Dayton but moved to an assisted living facility in a neighboring city to be closer to her daughter. Although she was a well-adjusted person, her initial adjustment in her new home was difficult. All signs of familiarity were gone. A visitor from the local parish recognized her situation and made efforts to bridge the gap for Betty. Between the visitor and Betty's daughter, they slowly introduced Betty to new stores, a new hairdresser, new doctors, and new friends. Either the visitor or a family member always accompanied Betty to each new place until she felt at home in her new surroundings.

Changes that lead to loss of independence can result in a tremendous sense of personal loss. Diminishing independence is a major loss in itself, regardless of what contributed to the diminishment. Generally, major contributions to diminishment of independence are through physical, social, and psychological losses that accompany aging. These include loss of hearing, sight, mobility, contact with family and friends, and the inability to participate in social activity. In addition to these losses, there may also be memory loss, the inability to carry on conversation, and the inability to remember the names and faces of those who were once familiar. All these and many more unmentioned changes challenge a person's ability to relate to others and often to care for himself or herself. Major adjustments to major changes often take longer for older adults. It may be difficult for younger persons who have not walked in the shoes of the older person, to understand the difficulty.

Letting go of so many persons, places, and things in a short period of time creates a real void. Replacements for some of the losses can satisfy the emptiness that comes from "letting go." New activities substitute for lost activities. New friends partially fill the gap left by lost friends. Often parish visitors who are aware of these losses can facilitate the process of making appropriate substitutions. This is done delicately, by first recognizing the loss and not minimizing it and recognizing too that the substitute is just that. It is a substitute and may never totally replace what was lost. Letting the elder know that the visitor understands the loss increases the trust level between them, and the elder is more likely to receive the suggestions for substitutions more easily.

While ministering to an elder, it is wise to remember certain things. Many elders have difficulty reaching out over and over again, especially in making new friends. Many have lost so many friends as they moved into their later years, they fear making new ones. They do not want to set themselves up for yet another loss. This is often difficult for a younger person to understand. Younger persons find it easier to reach out and make new friends and cannot easily identify with multiple losses until they themselves experience them. In each situation, it is wise to try to see life from the perspective of the person being visited. This lets the elders know they are a vital part of the relationship. It helps them feel important to the visitor just as the visitor is important to them.

Sharing a Mutual Ministry

Through mutual ministry, visitor and person visited enter into a partnership. In this type of relationship, the ministers not only serve others but allow themselves to be served. The following example occurred in a long-term care facility and illustrates this concept well.

Bill lives in a long-term care facility that is operated by a Catholic diocese. There is a beautiful chapel in the facility. Some of the residents gather in the chapel daily before lunch and pray the rosary together. One day eighty-eight-year-old Bill shuffled down the hall and stopped to see what was going on. A staff member told him that several residents were praying the rosary together. Bill started to enter the chapel to join them, but stopped short of going in. He said "You can pray too much you know. I think I'll go down the hall and visit a few people. I haven't thanked my housekeeper today yet, and she does a wonderful job of cleaning my room. I like to stop at the nurse's station and tell the nurses what a great job they are doing. And I need to stop at Al's room and see how he is doing. He hasn't been feeling well for a few days and I want him to know how much I miss him walking the halls with me." And Bill shuffled off to minister to staff and other residents in his own way.

Bill was in fact ministering to those who usually minister to him. He knew praying was important, but he chose to care for others at that time. In ministering to elders, it is good to allow them the privilege of ministering in return. This is done by accepting hospitality, by asking them to pray for the needs of the parish, by allowing them to assist when possible and feasible, and by learning from them important lessons of life, love, and forgiveness.

Appreciating the mutuality of ministry contributes to making the ministry of visiting elders more meaningful.

For Reflection and Discussion

» In what ways can you offer affirmation when you visit the elderly?

» How might a visit with an elder contribute to your own faith development? Give some examples.

» How would you feel about visiting a person with memory impairment? Do you believe he or she has a story to share?

» What is your concept of "a quality life"? How does one achieve a quality life? Do you know an elder who has done so?

» What changes have you observed as part of the aging process? How do these changes affect the people you visit?

» What are some ways to practice mutual ministry when you are visiting an elderly member of the parish?

CHAPTER TWO

The Ministry of Visiting Elders

Rose was active in her parish and local community for many years. In her later years, she moved to a healthcare facility because she suffered from crippling arthritis. Even though Rose had moved to a Catholic facility, she remained interested in attending Sunday liturgy and other activities in her former parish. Several parishioners formed a team and assumed the responsibility of taking turns driving Rose whenever she needed a ride. They also took turns visiting Rose, who continued in that way to be an active member of her parish. She remained connected to her parish because of these thoughtful and caring parishioners.

Responding to Elders

Rose's parishioners are a good example of a parish responding to the needs of elders. Chapter One provided reflection
and offered information to assist in understanding and
appreciating older adults. The stage was set for making the
visiting experience a viable one. Visiting an older parishioner
helps build a bond between the elder and the parish. It helps
make a connection that eases many lonely moments for persons who spend much time alone. Making a connection has
relational meaning.

Persons connect on individual, family, or community levels. For many older adults, belonging to a particular parish is
a primary connection for them. Through their early and middle years, this connection was often taken for granted. When
they became ill or otherwise incapacitated, the connection
weakened. For some, if there is no other way to remain connected, the connection may be completely broken and lost.

Visiting another person is one way of creating a bond. It is
helpful to know the person's interests and to understand his
or her personality traits. It is also helpful to know who are the
significant persons for them. If they provide this information to the visitor, it is beneficial. Otherwise, the visitor
should try to learn as much as possible from others who are
acquainted with the elder. Such information facilitates conversation and eliminates any unnecessary challenges.

Visiting our elders is a way of bringing hope and comfort
to them, especially if they spend much time alone. Spending
time together provides an opportunity to show gratitude to

the elders for their many years of service and participation in the parish and community. A visit provides a way of maintaining a vital connection between elders and the parish.

Bringing Hope and Comfort

A visitor offers hope to an older adult by affirming the elder as a valued member of the parish. Through such affirmation, elders feel that they are worthy of someone's time and capable of maintaining a connection with the parish. A visitor offers comfort to elders by walking with them on their journey with God. People who do not have company or any avenue for companionship often experience loneliness. They feel cut off from others. In a certain sense, loneliness is a part of each person's life, especially as each one has private experiences of which others are not a part.

It is wise to keep a healthy perspective when visiting a person who is sick or alone. Listening to and engaging in deep conversation builds a closeness between the involved persons. A deep relationship and possibly an attachment to the person can develop in a very short time. It is wise for visitors to remember that they are an instrument in bringing hope to the lonely and comfort to the sick, and that they are using their gifts to bring the elder closer to God. Visitors become a vehicle for helping elders grow closer to God. This kind of visiting involves a deeper sharing of the presence of God with others. Providing sufficient attention to elders is a way of showing gratitude for their many years of participation in a parish or community.

Offering Gratitude

In sharing the gift of God's presence during a visit, a spiritual connection can be made. During the time together, visitors will want to thank older adults for the many years of service and participation in the parish, either in their current parish or the one in which they spent their earlier years. Many elders helped build up their parishes in their early years, both financially and through volunteer work on many levels. They were active ushers, choir members, lectors, Eucharistic ministers, and they performed other often thankless duties, like counting the Sunday collection or cleaning the church. Some may have assisted with religious education classes or cared for little children so that parents of the children could attend liturgy free of distractions. Most were faithful in their attendance at liturgies and supported the church financially with their Sunday envelopes. Many of these services are often forgotten by others once a person becomes incapacitated and can no longer physically get to the church building. It is gratifying for older parishioners to realize that they are not forgotten. It is comforting to realize that somebody is grateful for who they were and what they did in their early years. This act is a vital part of the visiting ministry.

> Marie, an older parishioner, lives alone and is physically unable to get to church. However, she is vitally interested in the people and activities of the parish. Grace, a parish visitor, visits Marie often. She not only brings her a parish bulletin but keeps her posted on current parish activities. Grace often brings

pictures from parish events so that Marie can visualize the activities and the people. Grace also keeps Marie updated. If prayers are requested for children making their First Communion, Grace will take pictures of the children to Marie. This helps Marie feel that she is a vital part of the parish.

Older persons, especially those who once experienced a strong sense of belonging, often feel isolation when they are no longer highly involved in a parish. They search for ways to fill the gap that develops through times of lesser involvement. Parishioners and other leaders respond to these situations by recognizing elders as great resources and inviting them to contribute to the parish to the degree to which they are able. One example is by asking for prayers for the people and needs of the parish. As contributing members, elders are a resource for strengthening a parish as well as receiving life from it. All the above concepts are good to remember when engaging in a visiting ministry.

Listening Skills

One of the greatest gifts to use when visiting elders is the gift of listening. It is a discipline that involves observing, respecting the person, withholding judgment, acceptance, not minimizing needs, building in the confidentiality factor, clarifying and validating, and utilizing the power of silence. An expansion of these gifts follows:

> *Listening is a discipline.* It can be neither casual (hearing only what one feels like hearing) nor manipulative

(interpreting what one hears the way one wants to hear the message). A basic ingredient in listening is a respect for people and for their concerns. Listening allows the listener to better understand the speaker. If a person listens with ears, eyes, and heart, and hears not just words but the meaning and feeling behind the words, he or she is a good listener.

Listening includes observing. A person or family may tell a visitor everything is fine and they do not need anything. But your eyes happen to notice pantry shelves in the kitchen with little or no food on them. You may want to ask questions about this. When asking a question, give permission to withhold information. You can say something like, "Just tell me whatever you feel comfortable sharing. If there is anything you do not want to say, that is perfectly fine."

Listening involves noting what may not be obvious. Someone who lives alone can build up the illusion that there are many people in his or her life. This may be a cover-up for loneliness. If the person talks incessantly while the visitor is present, the visitor can assume that loneliness is indeed a factor. On your first visit, the elder may need to do all the talking. A relationship begins to form during your follow-up visits.

Listening includes acceptance, that is, meeting another person as an equal. If a visitor reflects the idea of sharing service, the dignity of the elder is enhanced. Many may be reluctant to receiving service unless they feel they are also contributing to the experience. It provides an even exchange for them.

Listening involves withholding judgment. A good listener puts the tendency to judge on hold and takes care not to make judgments about how a person maintains a home or about equipment they have or anything they may see that seems out of the ordinary. Enter a person's home or space with openness, compassion, concern, and interest. Enter another's space in the name of Jesus and in the name of the parish. Let elders know that if there is anything the parish can do for them, you would be happy to make it known to the appropriate person. Also, if there is anything elders can do for the parish, let them know what that is. Let them know how much their prayers are needed in the parish. Give some specific intentions for which they can pray: for children making First Communion, reconciliation, or confirmation, for a fund drive the parish might be having, or for those who are ill. At a follow-up visit, give an update on whatever intentions they prayed for.

Listening involves showing acceptance. No matter what the person is telling the visitor, it is important not to show disapproval. They may tell you their grown child is contemplating a divorce or a grandchild is thinking of having an abortion. If the visitor shows disapproval, this may deter the person from pursuing their concern and getting appropriate help from appropriate channels.

Listening actively encourages a visitor to refrain from minimizing the needs of elders. A need may seem minor to a visitor but may be a real need for an elder. Examples are getting their nails clipped or hair washed and combed, or getting bread and milk in the house. Jesus himself showed us how to serve others. He got a basin of water and washed the feet of his disciples.

Listening carefully builds confidentiality. It is vital that persons receiving a parish visit know and feel that what they share is not going to be heard throughout the neighborhood or parish. In fact, some may be more comfortable sharing with a visitor they do not know. Visiting and listening with an air of confidentiality encourages them to speak when they might otherwise be reluctant to do so.

General Perspectives

Besides the listening skills listed above, the following general perspectives will assist in making a visiting experience a meaningful one.

Ask what the person likes to be called. Some prefer Mr. or Mrs.; others prefer their first name or a nickname. Let the person know what you like to be called.

Speak clearly, in a low tone, and use shorter sentences. This method is good for memory-impaired and hearing-impaired persons. It is also good for those who are not in contact with people often and have limited conversation opportunities.

Adjust your speed of talking and reacting to the person's speed in responding.

Be more concerned with feeling and relating than with giving advice. Visitors are not present to provide counsel, but rather to support the elders and reassure them of their goodness and place in the community and parish.

Be present to the person. Speak and listen as though you are the only two persons that matter.

Avoid showing fear or apprehension. Elderly and/or sick persons are often alone much of the time, and they do worry that others don't visit them because they are difficult to be with or their illness is repulsive. Try not to show disappointment or disapproval.

Confidentiality is key. As delicately as possible, let the person know of your respect for confidences shared. It is important to refrain from sharing information shared with you in confidence.

Respect the elder's need to be in control, to be valued as a person, to avoid being a burden. This is helpful advice, especially if you disagree with something that is shared. Sometimes, however, if the elder is capable of carrying on a conversation, disagreeing on certain issues can be stimulating.

Listen to what the person is saying. Be affirming. Older or ill persons often wonder why they are in the condition they are in, and they ask questions about it. Affirm their fears and any anxiety by repeating the question, possibly in your own words. This lets elders know that you understand their fear and anxiety. Affirm them. Let them know that the condition they are in did not occur through any fault of theirs.

Alleviate any anxiety elders may have about their physical condition and what awaits them in the future. Try to understand where they are coming from and assure them that no one can predict the future.

Allow elders to express their feelings. Validate their feelings by letting them know it is okay to have them. Do not deny or try to change their feelings.

Allow the person to shed tears, and know that it is okay for you also to shed tears. Tears are another way of expressing feelings. They often alleviate fear and anxiety and release the buildup of pressure. They may also precipitate healing.

Take caution with words spoken aloud in the presence of those who are unconscious. They may be able to hear the words. If words are negative, they bring stress to the person. The stress is compounded because they cannot respond or defend themselves. If you speak aloud, say words of encouragement. Do not say any words you would not say if the person were conscious.

Being in tune with the needs of the person being visited lets the visitor know when it is time to end a visit. Do not prolong a visit, especially if the person is ill.

Persons who are not physically ill may appreciate a longer visit.

Share parts of your story without monopolizing the conversation. Such sharing helps broaden another's perspective and also gives the elder the privilege of caring for you. It also helps them feel they are reciprocating care and friendship by praying for you if they are able to do so. This provides an avenue for mutual ministry.

Refrain from passing judgment on another's life. What happened is history. Persons telling their stories need to feel validated, not rejected. Listen with care, support, and attention.

Know your place when visiting a health care facility. Support the staff that is serving the person you are visiting. Do not try to solve their problems. Assume that family and facility staff are doing what is right or best, unless of course there is something blatantly amiss. In a facility, follow whatever procedures are set up by the facility. Most facility staffs welcome suggestions. If you are a regular visitor, acquaint yourself with the staff and they will respect your suggestions.

Take care not to take too many gifts to the person. This is especially difficult for someone who is not in a position, either physically or financially, to reciprocate. A gift of prayer or a greeting card from time to time lets the person know of your love and care for them.

Look beyond old age, illness, or incapacity. See the spirit of the person. Set an atmosphere to let the spirit shine. Comment on any positive qualities the person has. Affirm them as much as possible.

It helps to *put yourself in the place of older persons* and test what your feelings might be if you were in their situation. Act accordingly.

If you have an aversion for older or sick people, do not offer to visit them. Try another ministry.

Communication Tips

Communicating with the memory-impaired brings certain challenges. In most cases, persons who are memory-impaired may be unaware of words they are using. If you were once familiar to them, they may or may not remember who you are, even if you are a relative or close friend. If they are meeting you for the first time, they may act like they have met you before. You may remind them of a former acquaintance and they make an association. Some persons who appear to be confused may not be confused all the time. Do not be alarmed with inconsistent behavior. It is wise to remain in the present as much as possible and not try to make corrections in perception. The choice of response is in knowing when to use verbal and when to use nonverbal communication. A combination of both is generally the best way to communicate.

Verbal communication tips

Face the person; make eye contact; call the person by name before speaking further. Know ahead of time what names they like to be called and what names they identify with for themselves. Tell them your name but do not be offended if they don't remember it or if they call you by another name. You may remind them of someone else.

Speak slowly, one idea or phrase at a time. It sometimes takes time for elders to process what you are saying. It takes even more time to interpret what they hear into something they understand.

Remain calm, no matter what response you get. This helps earn the person's trust. If you become agitated, expect the elder also to become agitated, or to tune you out completely.

Be patient. Give the person necessary time to respond to your comments or questions. Do not be shocked if the response is inappropriate or does not match the question at all.

Do not be argumentative. Even if you disagree, do not challenge the person verbally. Patience and understanding go a long way.

Be very clear with your statement or request. Do not use abstract words. Avoid being condescending. Calling a person "honey," or referring to them as if they were a child is condescending. Regardless of the memory-impairments, older adults have lived a long life with years of experience, and these are still a vital part of their identity.

Validate the person and the response. This lets the person know you got the message.

Encourage the person in a positive way as much as possible. Frequent acknowledgment in and of itself goes a long way.

Nonverbal communication tips

Use facial expressions and other gestures to accompany your words. Persons do recognize smiles and pleasant encounters. They also recognize unfriendly or unpleasant encounters.

Use some physical movements when helpful to reinforce your message. Use your hands, your arms, your body to support what you are saying. Supporting movements help convey your message.

Treat the person as your peer. Do not talk down or look down on another. Most persons can perceive if another thinks of them as being not fully grown or not capable of understanding what is being said. This includes memory-impaired persons.

Do not force a touch or physical contact. Some people are not comfortable with these. Touch safely, without personal interference. This is true when dealing with any person of any age. However, with some persons, a personal touch may be the only human contact they receive. For persons with poor vision, a human touch can be reassuring.

Position yourself on an equal or lower physical level with elderly persons. When they are in wheelchairs or lying in bed, sit in a chair that puts you equal level with them. It is overpowering for a person to try to communicate with someone who is towering over them.

As memory impairment progresses, functioning in the following areas may occur:

Short-term memory loss (persons may not respond appropriately). Try to be understanding. Try not to show frustration at the lack of follow-through in a conversation.

Short attention span (persons may not be able to follow a conversation). Be prepared to handle a change in topic several times during any conversation.

Confusion or disorientation. This requires a certain amount of patience and understanding.

Restlessness (persons may not be able to stay on one topic too long). This usually accompanies a short attention span.

Trouble with listening and understanding. Affirmation and reaffirmation can keep a conversation flowing.

Verbal expressions that do not make sense. Give simple responses that prevent elders from thinking they did not make sense.

Some frustration, anger, depression, especially if they do not understand what you are saying. Simple reassurance that it is okay not to understand everything may alleviate the situation.

Note that it is advisable at times just to sit quietly in another's presence. It is not necessary to have conversation flowing continuously during an entire visit.

In advanced stages of memory loss, persons often regress to the following behaviors:

» long-term memory loss

» inability to communicate with words

» personality changes, either long term or from visit to visit

(During the above three behaviors, a quiet reassuring presence is in order.)

» abusive behavior, to self or to others. Older adults may unknowingly address another inappropriately. They may use abusive language and not realize it. Please do not take the abuse personally. It may seem to be directed at the visitor, but usually is not. Most of the time, it is difficult to figure out why the elder acts or speaks in an abusive way. Quiet presence and silent prayer may help the situation. Do not respond to abusive behavior either in word or in action.

As mentioned previously, good communication creates a bond between persons. This bond keeps elder persons connected to the outside community, to the parish, to family, and to extended family.

For Reflection and Discussion

» Why do you think "connecting" is such a vital element in the lives of elders?

» How does the visiting ministry contribute to making connections in the lives of elders?

» What are some ways you can bring hope and comfort to lonely elders?

» What listening skills do you find most helpful when visiting elders? (Practice these skills with another parish visitor.)

» What communication tips in this chapter did you find most helpful? Why?

» What kind of visitor would you like if you were an elder? What qualities would you value?

CHAPTER THREE

The Visiting Experience

While visiting the home of an older parishioner, Nell had no preconceived notion of what to expect. The parishioner, Catherine, lived in her own home alone in a quiet middle-class neighborhood, but she kept to herself much of the time. So no one suspected that there might be a problem in her life. Catherine's sister lived in another state miles away. In several recent phone calls, her sister suspected that Catherine might be having some problems, even though Catherine said everything was fine. So the sister called Catherine's parish and asked if someone could visit her. The visitor learned that Catherine had not left her home in several weeks. She had eaten every last bit of food that was in her home. She was in a deep state of depression and did not know how to pull out of it. When Nell entered Catherine's home, she was shocked to see a house in total disarray.

Catherine's three cats had chewed her curtains and other pieces of furniture, probably due to hunger. Catherine was sitting at a card table, sipping her last can of soup. For some reason, she had a big smile on her face. Nell responded to Catherine's smile by relaxing and hiding her initial feelings of fear. At first, Nell was overwhelmed by all she saw and experienced. But she concentrated on Catherine's smile and was able to move beyond her shock and initiate what turned out to be a lengthy visit. With the help of a social worker from the local Catholic Social Service Office, they were able to provide an assessment and get appropriate help for Catherine. Nell went in as a pastoral visitor, encountered a woman in need, and followed through on getting appropriate social services. Eventually, she served Catherine as a pastoral visitor. This story may seem extreme, but it really is not so unusual. Similar stories about elders in need are uncovered when our eyes, ears, heart, and sensitivity lead us to them.

The main objective of a parish visiting program is to provide a coordinated visitation plan for older parishioners who are homebound and/or need supportive relationships to enhance their daily lives and to confirm their continuing membership in the Church. Through baptism, all Christians are called to participate in the life of the Church. Being a visitor is one way for parishioners to respond to this call. The baptismal call to service does not cease, however, when one reaches a certain age or becomes homebound or incapacitated. Elderly persons need to feel they too are participating in the life of the Church as much as or perhaps even more than active members. Elders and homebound persons need to feel the sense of belonging that being in a parish offers, especially since they cannot participate as actively. A visitor, especially from the parish, becomes a link, a vital connection that allows a homebound person to continue to belong to and serve the parish.

One value integral to a parish visiting program is "personhood," with emphasis on human dignity. This emphasis helps a visitor to focus on the spirit of elders, to recognize the presence of God in them, to call forth a response of faith, to share faith, to see beyond incapacity to the spirit alive within them.

Another visitation value is service. Jesus brought a deeper meaning to service by teaching that it is both essential for showing love for others and a distinct condition for following him. In becoming a visitor in a parish, you are following Jesus and also bringing credibility to his mission of love and service.

Another Christian value is community, which takes into consideration the basic needs of all human beings. Through a visiting program, homebound persons are provided with an opportunity to continue belonging to a parish and to share faith with the other members of their faith community. Through a visiting program, elders and other homebound parishioners are invited and welcomed to be active members of the parish, especially as powerhouses of prayer.

Guidelines for Visiting

Remembering that visiting is first and foremost a ministry, here are some guidelines for ministering to and with elders.

Imitate Jesus who promoted wellness in body, mind, and spirit.

Encourage whatever the elder needs to foster spiritual life. Incorporate a message of faith and prayer into each visit.

Represent the Church, which is a place of hope and healing, a place where people who are broken in body, mind, and spirit can go for healing.

Represent the local parish. Bring as much of a sense of community to elders as possible. When they cannot physically go to church, the visitor is the representative from the parish that goes to them.

Clearly explain the purpose of your visit. State who you are, who you represent, and why you are visiting at this time.

Show acceptance. Focus on the positive. It is possible that elders, especially if they live alone, may not be clean and neat. It is also possible that their houses have not been cleaned in a long time. Nevertheless, find something positive to talk about, like perhaps an interesting picture on the wall or a piece of antique furniture.

Specific Guidelines

Guidelines and suggestions previously mentioned apply, whether visiting an elder at home or in a care facility. They can also apply when visiting an elderly or ill person in a hospital. Some practical guidelines to be considered when visiting elders in more specific settings follow.

For Visiting Elders at Home

If elders are living alone in their own homes, a visitor may want to find out if there are special needs that require attention. This is especially true if the person has no immediate family or anyone who looks after their needs. These needs might include:

Meals. Are they able to cook their own meals? If so, who does the grocery shopping? If cooking and shopping are a burden, are they interested in getting home delivered meals? (Your local Council on Aging agency can direct you to the best delivery service in your area.)

Home Care or Home Health Services. Do they need assistance with housekeeping chores? Are there home health care givers who could supplement their health care? Would life line assistance be in order and offer some security?

These questions can also be directed to your local Council on Aging agency. (Call Elder Locator at 800-677-1116 to locate an agency in your area.) This agency will also have information about the availability of transportation for necessary appointments.

If an elder is living with a family member or another person, they may still have needs that require attention. In conversation, the visitor may want to make sure that vital needs are not overlooked. This is not always easy to recognize. One cannot assume care is being provided, even though there are persons in proximity to the elder. Other family members living with the elder may also need attention. Perhaps their own needs or lack of appropriate resources and services prevent them from providing necessary care for their loved one.

> Ann moved in with her aging mother in their family home. Ann is the only living child in the family and has no family of her own. She is the primary caregiver to her mother. Ann is in remission following treatment for cancer. Chances of recurrence of the disease are high, but Ann ignores the issue because her concentration is on providing excellent care for her mother. Ann also needs to be aware of community resources for herself as well as for her mother.

Try to discover if the person you are visiting is open to receiving help or learning more about available community resources and services. If you are aware of these resources, you can share the information with the family. However, they may need more information than you can supply. If the parish has a parish nurse or health care ministry, make the referral for the family, if they wish to be referred. If these services are not available on the parish level, use the above information on the Council on Aging services to make the contact. If the family prefers to make their own contact, allow them to do so. In no way should a parish visitor interfere with the family process. Give encouragement, but do not take over. However, it is good to get as much information as possible, to be aware of the family dynamics in each situation. Decisions made by elders who live with family members are often made in deference to the wishes of other family members, so as not to offend or lose them. Many older adults tend to downplay their own personal choices and preferences in such situations. This is good to know when conversing with elders.

Guidelines for Visiting a Health Care Facility

If the elder is living in a health care facility, follow any procedures set up for visitors in the particular facility. However, make your acquaintance and position as parish visitor known either to the charge nurse or to the social worker in the facility. The same procedure also helps for hospital visitations. A move to a new situation, especially to a health care facility, often challenges the elder's sense of trust and independence, even for those who are well-adjusted. Moving to a health care facility, even if it has an excellent service reputation, makes them feel stripped of strength and independence. A period of adjustment is to be expected, especially if the person experiences weakness from failing eyesight or hearing. These often influence their ability to communicate with other people and with the outside world. If their means of communicating are compromised, they also lose a sense of trust.

Many persons living in a care facility are chronically ill and many may have been in the facility for a long time. For some, the emotional needs may be greater than the physical needs. It is meaningful for them to see a fresh face, a friendly smile, and an understanding heart. When entering a person's room, make sure you are not interrupting a doctor, nurse, or nursing assistant who is attending the person. This is also important if the person's roommate is receiving attention from medical or other persons. If the door is closed, check at the nursing station before entering. A closed door or a pulled curtain may indicate a need for privacy.

Always introduce yourself to the resident, especially on the first visit. Make sure the person understands who you are and why you are visiting. Many elders may confuse a pastoral visitor with a social worker or other staff member. Do not assume the elder remembers you from visit to visit. Introduce yourself each time, at least until the elder recognizes you. It is important that they know you represent the parish. Always follow these simple guidelines.

Ask the person what they want to be called, and use that name. Let the person know what you like to be called.

Allow elders to talk. Be a good listener. Try to discover what their interests are. Incorporate them into the conversation.

If a person complains consistently, *try not to take the complaints too seriously.* If they persist, refer the complaints to the charge nurse or the social worker.

If the person does not want to talk or appears to reject you, *do not take it personally.* They may be transferring their anger with another person or with themselves to you, simply because you are present. Sometimes just sitting quietly and reverently with a person can bring comfort to them.

If the person exhibits loneliness or restlessness, *do not undermine their feelings.* Respond as you would to any other friend or acquaintance. Do not show pity. Do not be overprotective. Treat the person as you would want to be treated. Pray with them if they wish you to do so.

Be sincere. Show genuine interest. People can generally recognize phoniness.

Do not assist elders with getting in or out of bed or a wheelchair. If they wish to be moved, *ring or ask for assistance.*

Take care in bringing food to the person, unless you know their dietary needs and if they have trouble chewing or swallowing.

Do not visit a care facility if you are ill.

Keep all information about the resident or the facility CONFIDENTIAL.

Upon leaving, let the elder know you will be returning. If you cannot visit at the agreed time, call the person or the nursing station. Give a good reason for not keeping your appointment. The elder was probably anticipating your visit and looking forward to it.

Guidelines for Hospital Visitations

People who are hospitalized often share the following feelings and experiences.

Helplessness and loss of freedom. The person is confined to a strange bed surrounded by people they don't know. Their clothes are removed and they are given a strange wrapping to wear. They may have a roommate who is a stranger. They experience many personal restrictions, in particular, bathroom privileges. Everything seems unfamiliar. They may be put on a restricted diet and be served food with which they are not familiar. There is diminishment or loss of privacy, especially if they are exposed to many tests. The whole experience is depersonalizing.

Fear of the unknown. Most hospital patients do not know what to expect from doctors, nurses, or technicians. They may question or even fear results of diagnoses, tests, treatments, or other procedures. They may fear the outcome of tests. Their sense of trust is challenged.

Anxiety about the reason for hospitalization. Many questions arise: What is the name, nature, seriousness, or duration of the illness? Will surgery be necessary? How extensive? Is there cancer or another incurable disease present? Will there be pain? How much and can it be endured? Is a contagious disease involved that will limit visitors? Will they learn the truth? Will the pain be alleviated? Will their appearance change? Will other people notice a change and find it difficult to be with them? Will they lose their independence?

Separation from loved ones and other familiar people. This can bring or compound feelings of loneliness or homesickness. If the person has no family, concerns mount about available care following release from the hospital. Questions include: Will I be able to return to my own home? Where will I go if I cannot return home? Will someone help me with these major decisions?

A sense of guilt often accompanies hospitalization. Why did this happen to me? Is God punishing me?

Some, especially those who live in an unpleasant environment, may welcome their stay in a hospital as a relief from the misery of everyday life. Whatever the patient's situation, please keep these guidelines in mind.

» Do not enter any room where the door is closed without first finding out why the door is closed. Inquire at the nursing station.

» Notice and honor any "No Visiting" or "Isolation" signs on doors.

» If a light is on over the patient's door, do not enter until the attending nurse has taken care of the person.

» Let the patient take the lead in shaking hands.

» Whether sitting or standing, remain at eye level with the person.

» Don't burden the person with your own physical ailments.

» Refrain from responding to the patient in a negative tone.

» Do not visit someone in a hospital if you are sick.

» Do not prolong the visit, especially if the patient is restless.

» If the patient has a roommate, acknowledge that other person unless the curtain is closed for privacy.

» As a general rule, it is better to leave the room if a meal is delivered. The patient needs to eat and may be uncomfortable eating while a visitor is present.

Setting Up a Parish Visiting Program

In order for any program to run successfully and smoothly, there must be a qualified coordinator. This coordinator can be either a staff member or a volunteer who reports to a staff member.

Qualifications of a Coordinator

» Good working relationship with the parish staff.

» Understanding of, and some experience in working with, older adults and with volunteers.

» Knowledge of community resources and how to access them.

» Basic interviewing, organization, and supervision skills.

» Ability to communicate well, especially with older adults.

» Ability to maintain confidential information.

Responsibilities of a Coordinator

» To contact and screen prospective visitors.

» To accept referrals for parishioners who need or desire a visit.

» To interview the visitor and to visit the elder in order to set up a viable relationship.

» To assign visitors to referrals.

» To provide training, support, supervision, and evaluation of visitors.

» To organize and maintain records on both visitors and referrals.

Needless to say, all the information is collected only to facilitate a more meaningful visit and to ensure security and safety in case of emergencies. All information is confidential and should be used cautiously with respect to both visitor and the person visited.

Qualifications of a Volunteer Visitor

» An interest in, and understanding of, older adults.

» A positive attitude toward aging and toward persons who are ill or in some way disadvantaged.

» An ability to relate well with elders.

» A good listening ear.

» Time to visit on a regular basis.

» Ability to maintain confidentiality.

A commitment to be a volunteer visitor is made to God, to the Church through the parish, and to the persons being visited. The parish should provide the organization through which a visitor fulfills this commitment. Ongoing contact should be maintained between the coordinator and volunteer visitor. This happens through discussion and regular group meetings. During these communications, it is important to:

» recognize the place of older adults within the framework of the parish

» discuss commitment, expectations, and responsibilities of visitors

» identify skills in communicating with elders and other homebound persons

» clarify specific responsibilities

As part of this commitment, a visitor has certain responsibilities:

» attending group meetings

» visiting assigned elders and other homebound parishioners

» showing respect for persons served and value each as a person worthy of service

» communicating with the coordinator about vital information such as changes in procedure, time changes, inability to perform duties, changes in the homebound person that the coordinator or parish staff should know about, any disagreements that may have occurred and how they were handled

» having a love for and basic understanding of older people

» carrying out responsibilities well

To support the visitor in fulfilling responsibilities, the visitor can expect:

» to know in advance when meetings will be held

» to receive appropriate training and necessary information that contribute to a meaningful visiting experience

» to be regarded and respected as a vital member of a team

» to receive good communication from the coordinator, to be informed of changes in procedure and time, changes in the elder or homebound person, information on appropriate resources and support

The Program Itself

The coordinator solicits and trains volunteers and gives them a volunteer application packet. The packet should include an application form, an interview information sheet (to be used in assigning visitors), an agreement between the visitor and the parish representative, and a card to be used for filling out information on ongoing visits. The volunteer should also receive an elderly registration packet, which includes a registration form containing vital information on the person visited (to be used for emergency purposes or in the event a contact is needed), an interview information sheet, which provides a personal history of the person visited (to provide some background and promote conversation), and a card with information on the elder to be kept on file. Each parish should develop its own program and identify its own values. In the process, the coordinator and volunteer visitor are essential.

It's not easy to identify all the elders within a parish boundary, even those who need or desire a visit from someone in the parish. Sometimes these persons are identified if they experience a major trauma that causes them to be admitted to a hospital. If allowed by the Privacy Act, their presence in a hospital may be communicated to the parish. It may also be communicated when they are discharged from a hospital. Hospital staffs usually clear this process with the patient before communicating their presence to anyone.

Other ways to identify elders include keeping in touch with local service providers, such as police and fire departments. These officials are often aware of elders in their respective areas who live alone. Another way is to ask parishioners to be aware of their neighbors, and, without intruding on another's privacy, try to discover if the person has needs that require a response.

People who also have a family connection or strong neighborhood or community connections generally are not forgotten or lost in the shuffle. They are usually remembered if they were active in the parish or community before their illness. Those who are not as active do sometimes get "lost." Ask all members of the parish to be alert and help identify forgotten members of the parish and community.

A necessary element of visiting is a sense of commitment. Know the responsibilities associated with the visiting process, the time constraints, and the expectations. Commitment is essential. It is much easier on an older person not to have any visitors, than it is to think they are going to have a visitor who does not always show up or who does not seem interested in visiting. Emergencies do arise occasionally. When they do, communication to appropriate parties is essential.

It is a privilege and an opportunity to carry out a ministry within the church, especially one that continues the ministry that Jesus began and to which he gave a blessing. A visitor may be the bridge for someone to receive a long-awaited healing. A visitor needs patience, compassion, and sensitivity. If a visitor encounters a distressful situation, it should be discussed with the coordinator or other pastoral minister. If the visitor enters into a visiting ministry with a positive attitude, the energy will carry her or him a long way and will rub off on all other persons along the way, both those being visited and other visitors.

When going out to visit elders, go in the name of Jesus. Look at the situation as you think Jesus would. Treat each person as Jesus did. Listen as Jesus listened. Call on the Spirit to be your guide and inspiration.

For Reflection and Discussion

» Name some good reasons for having an organized parish visiting program. Are you willing to support such a ministry? Why or why not?

» Why is confidentiality such an important part of the entire visiting process?

» Which guidelines for ministering to and with elders would help you most as a parish visitor?

» When visiting elders in their own homes, what can you do or say to make them comfortable? How might you begin a conversation?

» Name some expectations a program coordinator might have of a parish visitor.

» Name some expectations a parish visitor can have of a program coordinator.

» Name some expectations an older parishioner can have of a parish visitor.

⊰§ CHAPTER FOUR §⊱

Response to Spiritual Needs

Following a major heart attack, John was hospitalized for several weeks. When Janet, a visitor from his parish, arrived, he lay in a semicomatose state. However, John seemed to be agitated. His face showed signs of discomfort. Janet tried to whisper some messages to him, but he remained agitated. Janet said a few spontaneous prayers, telling John that God loves him and wants to be with him. Yet he remained agitated. Janet did not know whether or not John heard or understood her. Finally, Janet began to say the Hail Mary. As soon as she prayed the words "Hail Mary, full of grace...." John quieted down. His face took on a look of calm, and he lay very still. It seemed that he heard words of a familiar prayer and responded in his own way. Familiar prayers centered him in the peace and comfort of God.

Spiritual growth can enhance the aging process, but it is often overlooked because the obvious physical diminishments demand attention and take precedence as a person ages. Yet people with a spiritual life are better able to deal with other aspects of aging. Spirituality encompasses the entirety of a person's life.

Older adults can often identify unique aspects of their spirituality, but these need continuous nourishment. The visiting ministry provides an avenue for this process to occur. Spirituality is a growth process. It is a movement within each person, at every age, but often it is more pronounced in older persons. Elders serve well as mentors for persons of every age. Visitors can learn from elders by being good listeners and giving the elder the freedom and support to grow to a greater wholeness. This is best done by affirming their lives, both past and present, and by supporting them as they deal with losses. It is also done by nurturing hope and keeping the movement of grace flowing within them.

This chapter deals with spiritual issues that affect the visiting ministry. These are the ministry of praying, refocusing energy, and dealing with lingering issues. Lingering issues often revive memories, and provide an avenue for reconciliation and for receiving God's grace.

Ministry of Prayer

The purpose of any prayer is to speak with and connect with

God. When we pray with our elders, we are helping them feel comfortable in God's presence and enabling them to speak to God freely. Words chosen should be words with which the elders are familiar, possibly words they may choose or which they have spoken about previously. Using familiar words often brings greater comfort, especially to those who are very ill. Most Catholics recognize the words of the Our Father and Hail Mary and through them they feel the comfort of the Lord or the Blessed Mother as they endure their suffering. These familiar prayers assist in building an atmosphere of peace and comfort with God that the sick or elderly person may not be able to maintain on their own at this point in their lives.

Guidelines for Praying

Ask elders if you can say a prayer with them. If the answer is "yes," proceed with a short prayer, or ask them if they have a favorite prayer. Ask if they want to pray aloud with you or if they simply wish to listen silently.

If the answer is "no," do not proceed with formal prayer. Simply remain present. Remind elders that God is pleased with them whether or not they speak words of prayer. Remind them that suffering with God and being in God's presence is prayer, and that God loves them as they are.

If elders wish to pray, begin with familiar prayers. Ask if they have a special intention for which to pray or a person for whom to pray.

Sense the timing and know when to pray aloud or when to remain in reverent silence.

God is a key partner in the prayer process. Faith allows one to recognize the presence of God in prayer. One first recognizes God. The words then, silent or spoken, express the felt relationship. This is true prayer. Through prayer, a vital connection is made with an elder on both a personal and spiritual level, and this can produce meaningful results. For one thing it helps them deal better with suffering and pain. As Christians, uniting their life experiences with Jesus brings them a tremendous sense of peace and comfort, especially if they are enduring much suffering.

Refocusing Energy

Elders who are suffering can refocus their energy by utilizing it for good. When elders experience a stroke, for example, their entire life is affected. People tend to judge them based on their physical condition. Physical weakness does not necessarily debilitate the whole person. Therefore, they need to be encouraged to develop their inner senses in order to refocus their energy.

Marcella, a resident in a long-term care facility, had many friends and always showed care and interest in them and in others in the facility. At age ninety-three, Marcella suffered a stroke that left her physically challenged and confined to a wheelchair. Because of her age and lack of mobility, most people

thought Marcella was affected mentally and spiritually. A nursing assistant, Sue, believed otherwise.
While assisting Marcella with activities of daily living, Sue realized that Marcella was fully aware of all
that was happening in the world around her. She
simply could not articulate her observations clearly
nor could she quickly respond or react to her observations. Through her patience and understanding,
Sue learned how to listen to Marcella and how to
translate her words and actions into responses that
made sense in many situations. It became clear that
Marcella still cared for her roommates and other
residents in the vicinity of her living area and that
she could relay their messages to anyone who had
time and patience to listen to her. Marcella became
the spokesperson for many who could not articulate
for themselves, and she lived her new role proudly
and with much love and care. Sue assisted Marcella
in refocusing her energy.

There are many ways to refocus energy. Believing that it
can be refocused in a positive direction is the beginning of the
process. Carrying out the belief makes the situation real.
Believing that God is part of the process and having faith that
God really wants the best for each person is the greatest blessing of all. Helping another refocus energy, especially as one is
near the end of life, is a special gift to another. When people
have time to think and reflect they are able to deal with any
lingering issues as they prepare to meet God. Often, these sur-

face when they realize that their time on earth is limited and they want to make peace with certain people or situations.

Lingering Issues

People often carry hurt and pain into old age, and these can be opportunities for spiritual growth. Very often, they have time and opportunity for hurts to be reconciled. At other times, this does not occur, and the pain lingers. The gradual lessening of physical power presents an additional challenge to such spiritual healing. Lingering spiritual pain is often worse than physical pains, great and numerous as they may be. Though opportunities for contact with a friend or family member with whom one is at odds diminish with age, there is still a need for forgiveness and this deepens with time. Memories of tension-producing incidents surface and resurface. Dealing with these memories, both bad and good ones, are important to a healthy, balanced spiritual life.

Memories

Memories connect our past with our present. Some elders participate in a life review, a universal mental process. They experience this process either formally or informally. When this happens, there may be an attempt to affirm the past and to find some meaning in life. This process can include an affirmation of the past and an enhancement of the present. It may then free them to move more freely and gracefully into the future. It is difficult to move on without a resolution of troubling images from the past.

At age seventy-nine, Hazel remained an active member of her parish and community. No one suspected that she was hiding a painful event that occurred earlier in her life. Following a near-fatal heart attack, Hazel managed to recover, but endured many physical challenges. Many people were surprised at how she hung onto life. None of her friends or family members suspected that she was covering up a situation that occurred many years ago when she lived in another town. Jeanne, a parishioner from Hazel's parish, visited her regularly following the heart attack. Hazel developed a comfort level with Jeanne and eventually shared with her the psychologically-debilitating experience she had in her early life. The event remained in Hazel's memory and affected her current life. Following a shared prayer experience, Jeanne noticed a change in Hazel's face and being. Hazel relaxed, became very calm, and her face glowed with peace. A week later, Hazel died quietly while sleeping.

When a visitor listens and affirms the healing process in another, the elder is able to move on. By allowing them to recall the incident and by asking appropriate questions, you can help the process of healing painful situations. Recalling the positive experiences of their lives with them helps them move beyond the negative experiences. By clearing up their inner vision, their blurred spots, they get a better perspective on their entire life picture. Healing comes when they have the sense of being heard and affirmed. They can't ignore negative feelings but with help can bring balance to negative memories and stir the need for reconciliation.

Reconciliation

While reflecting on life, older adults may highlight an area in which they feel regret and the desire to make reconciliation. They may also remember situations in which they think they may have failed someone. Pain can surface in relating the past. As hurts and pain are articulated, the relater often becomes more restful. The burden is lighter because someone else helps carry the load.

The bigger the list of perceived failures, the greater is the need for forgiveness. Children and younger persons generally have a shorter list. They experience forgiveness more quickly and often are rejuvenated by its power. But older adults often have difficulty with the process, because of the cumulative effects of failure and hurts. It takes them longer to experience the full impact that forgiveness brings. Articulating the experience to another and being affirmed brings relief and encourages movement to another phase of life.

Yet this kind of sharing takes time and trust. Recalling too many events at one time blurs an elder's inner vision. It becomes filled with painful emotions. Blurring keeps them from remembering the good things that happened. Recalling the positive experiences of life helps them to get beyond focusing only on what was negative. Clearing up the blurred spots puts their lives into better perspective. Healing comes when they have the sense of being heard and affirmed. Good listeners hear the good things and enter the conversation at appropriate times. The point is not to cover up negative feelings but to bring a greater balance to the situation. Listening sympathetically helps feed the spiritual life of the person sharing the story.

Pain is not always eased by forgiveness and often lingers after forgiveness takes place. Pain that lingers calls for the grace of God to make all things new. God replaces the brokenness with healing. Pain creates emptiness and hunger; redemption brings fullness and food for one's spirit. Healing of memories and reconciliation open a person up to receiving God's grace more fully.

God's Grace

The grace of God is active in both forgiveness of others and forgiveness of self. God offers to forgive people long before they forgive themselves. There is never a point in life when it is too late to receive God's gift of new life. It is vital to keep the movement of God's grace alive and to allow it to develop. God is a loving God who remains with us through the growth process and engenders within us a sense of peace and hope.

Carrying hurts into old age is destructive. Forgiveness is not easy, but is central to faith. As we grow older, it becomes difficult to make contact with someone who hurt us or someone we hurt. Many times, the hurt is carried for a long time, yet the person who seemingly inflicted the hurt goes on with life. That person may have long forgotten the incident. Or perhaps they were not aware of it in the first place.

Carrying hurts around for a long time only intensifies the pain. Forgiveness releases energy and relieves pain. Healing often eases memories associated with the hurt. Asking forgiveness and praying for those who hurt us are gifts. Accompanying another person in the process is a precious gift. These are signs of a true Christian. When Jesus felt forsaken, he did not stop loving those who hurt him. He prayed for them. Prayer leads us to our center, the place in our heart where God meets us as we are. Followers of Jesus allow those who hurt them to come into their center, so that God can touch both the person who was hurt and the person who inflicted the hurt.

Those who are near death, while refocusing energy, can successfully deal with such lingering issues. This experience prepares the person to go through the dying experience better prepared to meet God.

Questions for Reflection

> » Why is it good to use familiar prayers when praying with elders? What prayers would you propose for them?

> » What can a visitor learn by spending time with a person who is suffering? By praying with this person?

> » What did Jesus teach us about suffering? What specific teaching means the most to you?

» Name some ways you might help a person who is suffering to "refocus energy." Give some examples from personal experience.

» What part does forgiveness play in the life of an elder? What experience have you had of the need for forgiveness and reconciliation?

» How does healing of memories and reconciliation open a person up to receiving God's grace? How might you enable this?

CHAPTER FIVE

Suffering and Dying with Jesus

Lou taught in a Catholic school system most of his life. He enjoyed sharing knowledge with students. He taught English literature on a secondary school level and passed on to others the love of the arts and humanities. While still in his mid-fifties, he began to experience much physical discomfort. Several doctors told him nothing was wrong. Two different doctors told him to lose weight and all would be well. John knew something was wrong with him, yet the doctors did not support his feelings. Eventually, Lou went to a well-known doctor in another city. Following a thorough examination, the doctor explained that indeed a tumor was growing in Lou's body. They set a date for surgery to remove the tumor.

Shortly into the surgical procedure, the doctor's greatest fears were realized. Lou's body was filled with cancer. The surgery was not completed, since the cancer had spread to several vital organs. Lou knew something was wrong and was not totally surprised with the news.

Lou was not overt in his practice of religion, but was a quiet, spiritual man. His spirituality showed in his gentle manner of treating others, especially his students of many years. Lou was not a leader in his parish, but helped out with little things, like passing collection baskets at Sunday liturgies and delivering food and necessary items to families in need through the St. Vincent DePaul Society.

Following his surgery, Lou could no longer teach. He was very weak physically. But spiritually, he grew stronger, especially in his gentle, quiet ways. His former students and colleagues visited him often. They were touched by the graceful manner in which he accepted his condition. Many wondered what it was that kept Lou so peaceful. He did not exhibit fear, although he knew his time on earth was limited.

Although he did so quietly, Lou chose to suffer in union with Jesus. He strongly believed in life after death and chose to share his belief more by example than by words. Lou was comfortable in the house of the Lord during life, and knew he would be comfortable in God's house into eternity. Lou had taught

many lessons for years. Now he taught a different
lesson about living life in peace with God.

Suffering in Union with Jesus

Suffering is often accompanied by fear. This is especially true
for those who have endured much pain and loss in their lives.
However, even with the experiences of loss, many elders continue to pray. They maintain meaning in life by looking at it
differently than they did in their younger years or years of
better health. When a sense of purpose prevails, it provides a
positive lesson for others about how to suffer and how to
accept loss and pain. It shows that physical illness does not
necessarily prevent a person from being a model of wellness.
It helps to put all the events of life into proper perspective,
and it teaches others the value of a spiritual life.

There are many ways to express spirituality. Many elders
are expert in living a spiritual life and in showing how to do
so. Some express their spirituality overtly in an obvious and
magnetic way. Others live their spirituality quietly as an inte-
rior activity. They portray their spirituality by example
rather than by words. Allowing God's presence to live within
them and to recognize God's presence in others is a great way
to express spirituality.

Loss and change can be a source of suffering, as they often
blur one's view of life and distort one's perspective. We cannot predict what may happen throughout life. We can, however, maintain a relationship with God through each experi-

ence and event of life. Even as the body fails, the spirit of the person remains alive. Each person has the power within to maintain the necessary balance between body, mind, and spirit, in order to feel the balance between fear and hope, between negative and positive forces, between needs and blessings. At times, this power may be triggered by someone other than the person who suffers, for example, a family member, friend, or parish visitor.

The presence of another person, a visitor or friend, often fills a void created by the isolation that accompanies suffering. To those who suffer, it is comforting and healing to have another person walk with them. It is comforting to have their suffering acknowledged. When in the midst of pain, it is difficult to see any value in suffering, for pain often obscures a person's perspective. When a visitor recalls how Jesus handled suffering, this can inspire the person to suffer in union with him. It is a challenge and a privilege to walk with a person who suffers.

Jesus: Model of Suffering

Jesus was a prime example of how to suffer and how to walk with others who suffer. He modeled for us how to incorporate suffering into our lives. It takes great faith to suffer in union with Jesus. It takes great faith to walk with one who suffers in union with Jesus. Faith does not alleviate suffering, but it does assist a person in handling it. Bonnie was a living example of how to suffer in union with Jesus. Bonnie lived in a health care facility. The following conversation took place between her and Marge, a pastoral visitor from the local parish. It occurred about a week before Bonnie's ninetieth birthday.

Bonnie had been blind for about five years, but now in her ninetieth year, she was also dealing with terminal cancer. She managed to spread peace and joy to all around her, in spite of the intense pain she continuously felt. Having been confined to a wheelchair for several months, she was now confined to bed. Even moving one muscle was extremely painful.

Marge visited Bonnie about a week before her ninetieth birthday. Bonnie was deep in thought. She said to Marge "Do you think I'll make it?" To which Marge replied "Make it to what?" Bonnie replied "To my ninetieth birthday." Knowing of her intense pain and not wanting her to suffer more than she had to, Marge said "You know, Bonnie, I heard God throws wonderful birthday parties." Bonnie seemed to like that idea, but did not say anything. Marge sat quietly for awhile, then left so Bonnie could sleep.

Because of Bonnie's condition, Marge returned to visit her the next day. Bonnie lay very quiet. She seemed to be in deep thought. Marge asked her if she was afraid. Because if she were, Marge would stay with her through the night. Bonnie's face lit up radiantly, and she looked directly at Marge, even though she was blind. And she said "Fear? Why should I fear? My heavenly Father, who has cared for me all my life, is waiting for me. He is so kind and loving and merciful. Why should I be afraid?" Marge remained silent and remained with Bonnie through the evening.

Later in the evening, Bonnie opened her eyes again and said to Marge "What about you? Are you afraid?" Marge was surprised by the question, but simply answered, "I really don't know, Bonnie. I have not had a chance to prove whether or not I am afraid to die, so I don't know." And Bonnie's last words were "You won't be." She then gently closed her eyes and, shortly after, did go to meet her loving heavenly Father. And she did spend her ninetieth birthday at one of his grand welcoming parties!

Bonnie witnessed for Marge a true belief and hope in life after death. By the presence of God within her, she challenged Marge to respond at a deeper level. Bonnie ministered to Marge as Marge ministered to her. She believed in life after death and inspired Marge to hope in life after death. Bonnie exhibited the power to choose a positive path, even in the midst of suffering.

The Power to Choose

Even in suffering, we have the power to choose. People who are suffering choose to let the Spirit live in them. They can choose to rise above the suffering and overcome the physical and psychological challenges that accompany suffering. They can choose to let suffering be the focus of life and an entry into a fuller life. They can choose to use suffering to manipulate those around them, to inflict guilt on others, or to demand that others drastically change their ways for the benefit of the one suffering. They can choose to overpower suffering with love and with positive energy. They do not choose to suffer but can choose the response to it.

Suffering is not humanly desirable, yet it is part of life. It can be a grace to walk with another who looks at suffering and death openly and experiences the hope of beginning a new life with God. Real joy and peace rarely come without passing through some suffering. Jesus not only taught this but showed it by his example.

Dying in Union with Jesus

All life experiences can help fulfill the purpose of our existence: to be born of God, to live a life serving God, to die with God, and to live eternally with God. Most elders face death more gracefully than those who walk with them and who watch the process of dying. Most older adults are more realistic in facing death than younger persons. If they have had the opportunity to bring closure to significant relationships and have handled difficult situations well throughout their lives, they are more likely to face death with a sense of peace.

If elders have trusted God in situations throughout their lives, they are more likely to trust God in the final act of dying. Faith in God can be a powerful help when dealing with loss and grief.

Facing the Reality of Death

Parish visitors often face the reality of death and dying with an aging or sick person. In doing so, pastoral visitors also confront death in themselves. They face their own death while at the same time entering a bereavement process at the loss of someone they know and love, or have come to know and love through the visiting ministry. To be present to another through the dying process and into death is a holy experience. It is an opportunity to look within oneself, to see how the death of another can be a life-enhancing experience. It is also an opportunity to look death squarely in the face. Unless pastoral visitors deliberately choose to tune out the process, they recognize death as it affects life, their lives, and the life of the dying person. Life and death are part of a continuing process of growth and development. Dying and death, the ebb and flow of all life, offers many lessons to the living.

Most older adults have faced death numerous times, especially if family and friends have predeceased them. With each death experience, they were also forced to look within themselves. For those who concentrated only on the loss, the experience may have been more difficult. For others, who recognized the patterns of life and death, death becomes part of an ongoing life process. This does not mean they do not grieve. It only means they have a different perspective on death.

Through my many years of ministering to and with older adults, entering into life and death experiences has been a vital part of my ministry. Gradually, I grew from looking at death through my own eyes to viewing each person's death through their eyes. I have tried never to project my feelings onto the older person's situation.

While ministering in a long term care facility, the usual procedure when a resident died was to announce the death to other residents, so that they could pray and experience the loss together. Often, we had the viewing and funeral liturgy in the facility chapel. Many residents rejoiced with and for the person whose funeral we were celebrating. I, being much younger at the time, looked at death differently, gradually learning to view it through the eyes of the elders. One incident drove this home clearly to me.

Before Minnie died, I spent much time with her and with her son and daughter-in-law, and with those residents who were very close to her, ones she knew well and with whom she shared quality time. When Minnie died, her son and I were with her, and she died peacefully. But, before the announcement of her death was made to the residents, which we did by placing a notice on the clock outside the chapel, I tried to be sensitive to her best friend Henrietta, by telling her before she read the notice. I went to Henrietta's room to break the news to her gently and to prepare for whatever response she might make. I eased into it by saying "Henrietta, you know how sick Minnie has been and how she has suffered and, well, her suffering is now over and Minnie is with God." And Henrietta's response was

"Lucky Min! She finally died! Lucky Min! Maybe I'll go soon too!" As close as they were and as much as Henrietta knew she would miss Minnie, she rejoiced with her. She was quite open with her response. I was shielding myself. Henrietta did not need shielding. She needed support and understanding.

This is not to say Henrietta was not affected by her friend's death, but her response indicated that the encounter with death often changes for many as they age, and their perspective on life also changes. This perspective affects ministry to those elders who are facing death.

As persons age, time and energy is spent on maintaining balance in their lives: balancing fears and hopes; balancing negative forces with positive forces; balancing losses with appropriate substitutions. Many have power within themselves to do so successfully. Others need assistance from supportive and understanding persons to maintain a comfortable balance. In ministry to elders, pastoral visitors can supply the necessary motivation for elders to activate their inner resources and promote a healthy inner balance. Pastoral visitors can call forth gifts in elders, gifts they possess and use in both sickness and health, and even at death. It is more difficult to minister with/to elders in death if the visitor has not walked in their shoes in life situations. It is helpful, as much as possible, to delve into the person's personal history.

A visitor can get some idea of an elder's history from relatives and longtime friends. During a prolonged illness, it is easy to forget that history. But in hospitals, long-term care facilities, or even in person's homes, remember that the person in our presence has a unique past and contributed to making the parish, city, and environs a better place for the following generation. Sometimes we may learn what that history is through sharing and reflecting. At other times, the visitor may have to imagine that history. The important thing is that visitors maintain the relationship as they walk with the person facing dying and death.

Suffering and Dying

The intense suffering that sometimes precedes death can make the dying process appear to be the "final act" of living on earth. But dying is not just the final act. It is experienced throughout life, each time one faces a major change or suffers a significant loss. The grieving process accompanies each act of dying. Participation in the grief process throughout life is a preparation for the final act of acceptance, of death, and moving on to meet God face-to-face. For Catholic Christians, the sacrament of the sick can bring peace and comfort in the final moments of life.

Sacrament of the Sick

Sickness often separates a person from the community. For Catholic Christians, the sacrament of the sick brings the support of the Christian community and bestows spiritual and sometimes physical healing to the sick person. The rite was formerly given privately to those who were in danger of death. For that reason, it was called Extreme Unction, meaning last anointing. Currently, representatives from the parish community are often present for part of the ceremony. This sacrament brings the power of Christ and the comfort of the Christian community to the person facing serious sickness, surgery, or advanced age. It also offers the forgiveness of sins.

The sacrament of the sick raises the question of the meaning of life. There is no real answer to the mystery of human suffering. But the ritual helps the sick person recognize that suffering can be a participation in the mystery of Christ's death and resurrection. It requires an act of faith that allows the person to grow closer to God. The sacrament aims at strengthening and healing the whole person. The grace of the sacrament often helps the person to overcome feelings of anxiety and the fear of dying alone.

Questions for Reflection

» Name one way you might encourage an elderly person to suffer in union with Jesus.

» Do you believe there is value in suffering? How might you gently convey the value to one who is suffering?

» In what ways is Jesus a model of suffering? How might you best relay this message to a person who is suffering?

» Do you believe that a suffering person has "the power to choose"? How might you convey this to one who is suffering?

» Do you find it easy or difficult to be with a person who is dying? Why? What dictates when to speak, what to say if you speak at this point, and when to remain in reverent silence?

» Does the grieving process occur in a person's life only at the time of death? At what other times might a person experience grief?

∽§ CONCLUSION ᘒ

It was both difficult and easy to write this book. It was difficult because there were virtually hundreds of elders who entered my life through the years and each has had a precious story to share. Whose would I choose? On the other hand, it was easy because there are many common threads in their lives that together weave a beautiful, meaningful tapestry: stories of faith, hope, love, strength, forgiveness, and coping amidst adversity.

Myriads of elders continuously encourage and call forth life from me. They taught and teach me:

» How to live and how to die;

» How to enjoy pleasurable and simple times, and how to deal with difficult times;

» How to find some perspective in any life situation;

» How to laugh and how to cry;

» How to truly "let go" and trust in God.

Although the focus of this book is on the ministry of visiting and praying with elders in an organized setting, the information and suggestions can be helpful in any setting: family, neighborhood, and community. There are virtually thousands of older adults in our parishes who are aching to share their stories with someone who has time to listen. Look around your own parish and neighborhood and initiate a conversation. Share a story of yours. Listen. Show interest. You will make someone happy and fulfilled, and you too will be enriched.

The aging population is growing significantly in our parishes. Parish visitors can be the eyes, ears, and heart that connect them to the parish community. They can bring the message of Jesus to those who long to hear it in the waning days of their lives. Would you consider joining their ranks?